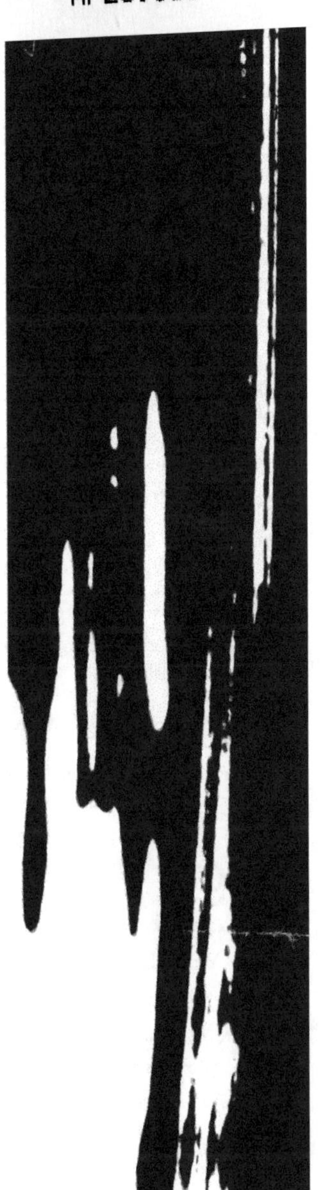

QUITTER

KEN VAN LIEW

CHANGE YOUR THINKING, CHANGE YOUR LIFE

BEYOND
PUBLISHING

New York. Los Angeles. London. Sydney.

ISBN: 978-1-63792-395-5 - paperback
ISBN: 978-1-63792-394-8 - hardcover
Library of Congress Control Number: 2022922491

CHAPTER
1

Jack woke up with a jolt, sitting upright, dripping in a cold sweat. His bedcovers were tangled as if he'd been in a wrestling match. But no, he hadn't been fighting. Instead, it was the same old dream. A familiar scenario. He was being escorted to the office doors, a box of his personal effects in his arms, accompanied by two security guards. The only difference was — this time —he was the one who had quit in a moment of bravado.

Jack lived in fear of that kind of dramatic change. He also feared the rapidly shifting economy, his failure to move up the corporate ladder, and his age. At 46, he was certifiably middle-aged. And it worried him, along with a slew of other troublesome issues. He looked over at Darla's side of the bed, hoping for some comfort. She wasn't there. She hadn't been there for nine months now but he tended to forget in the morning, expecting her to be right there. His darling Darla left, taking their kids, Harry and Heather, with her.

For 17 years they'd built a life together. He provided, while she took care of the kids and raised them well with manners, kindness, and all that goes with it. Then one day, Darla an-

nounced she was leaving him. The reasons he'd heard before — but he never took them very seriously. Lots of crying occurred. Mostly from the kids, as he would later learn. Some from Jack. But not Darla. She was stone cold and rigid.

Jack dressed and headed for the office. It was cool for this time of year, and the dreary drizzle only made the grass happy and the roads slick. A pallor of gray covered everything, which reflected his mood perfectly.

Jack's car rolled into his marked parking spot and he trudged towards the front door of his workplace. He was in such a rote state he barely even knew where he was. Even the route to work was a blur. He didn't remember getting there. The turns and stoplights and yields were so second nature his muscle memory got him to work each day without a thought. His cellphone rang, shocking him back into awareness.

"Hello?" said Jack, taken aback. The only people who ever called him were his immediate family. Perhaps the school if the kids are sick.

But it was his boss. "Jack, it's Arthur, how far away are you from the office? We're getting behind on this bridge project and need everyone firing on all cylinders." Arthur was former military, a drill sergeant no less, a strong personality who had little patience with "the weak." Arthur must've loved the military, Jack thought, because ordering people around came so naturally. Jack didn't particularly like the guy, but Arthur was his boss, so Jack did as he was told.

"Five minutes, maybe a bit more, less than ten," said Jack.

"Make it faster if you can," said Arthur, and he hung up.

Jack started for the elevator bank. Why not splurge today and get a fancy coffee? Sure, Arthur was waiting. Jack wasn't in the mood today to get shoved around.

Jack had been in the overpriced coffee shop in the lobby three times in all the years it had occupied the ground floor space, snotty the Baristas and all. Every time he ordered a drip coffee — black, two creams, one sugar — the guy taking his order got his name wrong, calling him 'Mack' instead of "Jack." Maybe it was some kind of practical joke they played on customers from time to time but, still, it was annoying as hell

Their coffee was good, he had to admit, but parting with $6.50 for a latte with frothy milk went against the grain like rubbing a porcupine backwards. Still, he indulged. Latte in hand, Jack headed to his office – finally, a real office with walls and a door and a good chair — a serious upgrade from the cubicle he'd occupied most of his career— and plopped down.

Michael walked by. Michael reminded Jack of good ol' Charlie, the man who changed his life by introducing him to his darling Darla. Michael and Jack had become fast friends when they were on the same team for a major highway interchange project a few years back. Michael was brash, quick with a joke and always bought the first round of drinks after work.

"Jack, dude, you look like death warmed over!" said Michael.

"Gee thanks, bud," Jack shot back very aware that, yeah, he looked like, well, death warmed over.

"Seriously, not trying to be mean but... have you even slept in the last few days?"

"Not much," said Jack. He didn't bother trying to hide his sadness. Not with Michael, who knew how badly the marital situation bothered Jack.

"Look, if you ever wanna get together, hang after work, grab a beer or something, just let me know and I'm there," said Michael, understandingly. After a beat, Jack nodded.

"Thanks."

"Of course, I'll have to get a signed note from my wife to attend," said Michael. Jack chuckled. That brightened his dreary morning, but only for a moment, as Arthur came in, wearing his usual scowl.

"Hemet, need you in this meeting. We're finalizing our bid for the Barrister County highway project and I have to have your input. Hey, you feeling alright? You look like crap. Splash some water on your face before you come to the meeting. Don't want our potential clients thinking we are running on empty," Arthur said, walking off briskly.

But Jack was running on empty. Down in the dumps. Didn't a guy whose life was falling apart have the prerogative to have a bad day?

Jack went to the restroom, splashed some water on his face and chugged the rest of his overpriced latte. He felt revived , but that was probably just the caffeine talking.

Jack's run-of-the-mill day continued. Meetings. Lots of meetings. More meetings. A restroom break where he stayed way too long trying to text Harry. Jack's son went to a school where the principal made all students put their phones in a bin until end of day. Jack knew it, but the yearning to connect made his stomach tie up on knots. He had never wanted to give a third grader a phone. All the other kids had one, and he didn't want Harry feeling left ou, the way Jack had felt left out most of his life.

Back at his desk, Jack looked at the clock. Almost time for lunch. He thought of lunch as a time to work and eat, a *duo of discipline* that made him more efficient that his collogues. Jack loved efficiency. Today, however, felt different. After all, he'd already bought a ridiculously overpriced coffee, so why not go in with both feet?

"I'm going out for lunch. Anywhere. I. Want," he said to himself, punctuating the last three words loud enough that someone might hear. No one heard him. Nor did they care about his lunch choices. Truth be told, most of Jack's workmates would be happy for him to take a leisurely lunch so they could ease up a bit and NOT have to listen to their boss's monotonous *be like Jack* speech.

Just as Jack was walking into the elevator lobby, Arthur walked by carrying a large stack of files.

"Where ya going, Jack ol' boy?" said Arthur.

"Out to lunch," said Jack, barely able to contain how he felt.

"What? You choose a day like today to not bring a lunch?" said Arthur, as if Jack was openly defying him.

"Day like what day?" asked Jack, truly perplexed. Arthur exhaled and rolled his eyes as if explaining something to a child.

"Look, you know this stuff. Carlos is out, he had a doctor's appointment or dentist or something like that, and Michael has to leave early for an event he has over in Worthington, so you're the man," said Arthur, smiling. He started to leave, then stopped before walking away.

"I'll drop all these on your desk, and I need them by the end of day. Order up a sandwich for yourself from the cafe downstairs, on me. Their chicken salad isn't half bad." Arthur disappeared around the corner. Jack just stood there, motionless, slack-jawed, not believing what he had just heard.

Normally, he would have turned around, gone back to his desk and dug in his heels for a long, difficult day. Today was different. Maybe it was the dream, the nightmarish scenario where he quit, or was he fired? He dreaded both situations. Perhaps the dream was just his deep-seated fears playing out? None of that mattered to Jack at the moment. He just wanted to get out of the office that had suddenly become a suffocating place.

"Screw him," said Jack under his breath. And he left.

CHAPTER
2

Jack was in his car and driving before he could change his mind. Normally, if he felt overwhelmed, he'd stop at the car door, reconsider, remember his duty, and return to work. Today, though, he couldn't get out of the parking lot fast enough. He was smart enough to turn off his phone, since he expected several angry messages from his big, bad boss. But Arthur, off on a long lunch with his brother-in-law, didn't even notice Jack was AWOL.

Jack drove around aimlessly. He passed several fast-food chains. But they were bland. Tasteless. Then a thought popped into his head. What about that deli he had always liked? Where was it exactly? Somewhere in Queenstown, which was at least 15-minutes away. But Jack didn't care about the distance. Not today. He headed east–

And then he heard it. Like a sign from the heavens. His song. The song of his youth. *It's My Life* by Bon Jovi, screaming to life on the oldies station. The mantra for every guy his age, every guy who came from a hardworking, middle-class American family. A song of self-reliance. Freedom. Doing things your way. Jack cranked it up, singing at the top of his lungs,

badly off-key, but with joy. He punched the air on the chorus. "It's! My! Life!" He felt like stopping the car and running the rest of the way (probably the caffeine talking the double shot the barista had given him.

When Jack arrived on Queenstown's main drag, the deli he loved was right there. Big Tony's. Jack smiled and found a parking space. The crowd had thinned a little, it was close to 1:30 when he opened the front door. A sense of calm came over him the minute he stepped inside. He savored the deep, delicious smells, the hum of happy people, the familiar cadence of people ordering their favorites. Jack felt he was home, almost. Now it was his turn at the counter.

"Hey Jack," said Big Tony, "Haven't seen you in ages. How's it going?"

"Fine, fine, how're the wife and kids?" replied Jack.

"Everyone's terrific, thanks for asking. Little Tony is about to graduate from high school, can you believe it?"

"Yeah, hard to believe how fast they grow," said Jack. He tried to push down the twinge of emotions, but Big Tony had always been a pretty intuitive guy.

"Hey, what's the matter?" asked Tony with concern.

"Yeah, nothing, I just, I miss my kids."

"Oh, uh, where'd they go?" asked Tony.

"To live with their mother…" A long pause. Jack couldn't meet Tony's eye, but managed to mumble, "she left me." Tony stopped everything, compassion behind his eyes.

"That's rough my friend, rough. Tell ya what, any order, on the house and, hey, I need a break, mind if I come sit with you?" said Tony. Jack was surprised and more than a little embarrassed.

"No, no, no, Tony! I'm not looking for sympathy! It's all my fault, all mine." Jack trailed off.

"It's never only one person's fault." For a second, Tony pointed a stiff finger at Jack, as if to console and cajole him simultaneously. Then he smiled, "So what'll ya have?"

"Meatball sub, and a bag of chips, but I insist–" Jack fumbled for his wallet

"Your money's no good today, my friend. Comin' right up!"

Jack ate with great gusto his beloved meatball sub, a full meal on a hunk of Italian bread made by Tony's bakers every day. He loved the "ultimate sandwich" almost as much as he loved its inspiration, Joey Tribbiani on *Friends*. He ordered meatball subs whenever he could, considering himself a connoisseur. Big Tony's were probably the best he'd ever had.

He was about to take his last bite, happy that Tony seemed to have forgotten his promise to sit and talk, when suddenly Tony plopped down in the booth across from him. Tony was usually blunt, quick to the point, and today was no different. "So what the hell happened?" Jack shook his head. How could he explain where and when his obsession about work had begun, his intensity about always being the go-to-guy and never quitting. And then, he remembered.

CHAPTER
3

Thirty-five years earlier, 11-year-old Jack was working himself into a serious sweat on the basketball court. Just when he was about to puke, Coach Jessup called out to him.

"Hemet! Sideline!" he shouted, gesturing for Jack to head to the bench. The boy hung his head. He'd done his best, but it wasn't enough. His best was never enough to match the skills of his teammates, not even at a practice scrimmage like this one, with the first team versus the rest of them. Jack knew his size, vertical leap and shooting skills left much to be desired.

"On the bench, son." Coach Jessup was a gruff man of 40 who seemed a lot older and had to be obeyed But Jack didn't sit. It was time to move on. Basketball was not the sport for him. Maybe archery? Or track? He was a good middle distance runner, and maybe a team sport wasn't for him. But he could hear his stepfather's expected response screaming in his ear. *Once a quitter, always a quitter!* His mom, though, she'd listen to him. He knew it. She'd say it was perfectly okay to walk away and find something better suited to his build. His determination was never in doubt. But

sometimes you just got to, *know when to hold 'em, know when to fold 'em.* All this ran through Jack's mind — and he folded.

"Coach," said Jack, approaching the man.

"What?" he replied without looking down at young Jack.

"I think, well, I think this is, uh, not the sport for me. I'm gonna focus on, uh, track I think, yeah, track, maybe the 800 or the mile?" said Jack and waited patiently for a response. Coach Jessup looked down, glaring at him, towering over the boy who was smaller than most his schoolmates. He said nothing for what seemed like at least two hours but was probably closer to 45 seconds. Then he cleared his throat and stooped to meet Jack in the eye.

"Yeah, well, go ahead and do what you gotta do," he said with unmasked disgust, "But remember this. You quit now, and you'll be walking away from every difficult task or tough situation for the rest of your life. So go on, get out of here…. quitter!" Coach Jessup waved the boy away. Jack just stood there, stunned. The coach had already turned his focus to his players on the court. Jack was no more than an afterthought. He left the gym quickly.

That night, young Jack was bewildered at the coach's outrage at his quitting something he obviously wasn't good at. As he lay down for to rest, after he'd recited his prayers, Jack had a hard time drifting off to sleep. He thrashed about until the covers were almost on the floor. Frustration flooded his mind because he could NOT stop hearing the words of his coach It was as if a chorus of voices was saying over and over and over: *"Once a quitter, always a quitter."*

From that moment on, Jack vowed aloud that he'd never be a *quitter again.* Quitting was no longer an option.

Back at Big Tony's deli, Jack's mind was clearly elsewhere for a few moments. But Tony was patient. Finally, Jack looked up. "What the hell happened? Good question, I don't want to bore you with the detail, I know you're busy."

"Forget about it, I'm the boss, and if the boss doesn't wanna be busy for a while, he can," said Big Tony, "And you don't have to tell any details that make you uncomfortable."

"Well, here's what happened, blow by blow" said Jack. He took a deep breath.

CHAPTER
4

Jack remembered the day she left down to the very last excruciating detail. He got home later than expected that night, having stayed until almost 11:00 pm. He arrived home at 11:15, thoroughly exhausted. But when he opened the door, Darla was standing in the hallway, waiting up for him. Very odd. And she was wearing her favorite grey and blue speckled cardigan, kind of her *I'm going out casually dressed'* outfit. Her arms were crossed, and she didn't even look up to meet his eye.

"Oh, hey, you're still up," said Jack, as he tossed his keys in the entry hall dish.

"We need to talk," she said. "You might want to sit."

"What's going on? Did something happen to one of the kids?"

"No. I mean yes. Well, uh, this isn't easy but the thing is. I'm leaving you. We're leaving you," she said, pain in every word.

Jack was dumbfounded. He stepped back as if hit hard in the chest. He sat.

"I don't understand, but, I, uh, why?" said Jack, as he racked his brain for his marital and

family sins.

"I've had it. I've been patient. I've begged and pleaded and asked nicely a thousand times but you just won't give up your mistress."

Jack jumped to his feet. "What?! Are you nuts? I have no mistress. Who has time for a mistress!?"

"Slocum & Grey Civil Engineers. Your job, that's your mistress. You put her over us time and time and time again, year after year. Always waiting and hoping to ascend from middle management to upper management. Always thinking that when that day comes, you'll be able to slow down. But by the time it does, if it ever does, the kids will be gone and married. I will not wait that long. And I will not ask again. So we are done," Darla spat out.

"But, but, what about the kids? They need their Dad, too."

"They do, but Dad's never around. Just so you know, they cried and cried when I told them. Hope you're proud of that. Because they do love you. Bottom line? They don't know you, and you don't know them. By the way, you missed Heather's recital tonight. Her first one! And she was brilliant and – you missed it. You'll never get that chance again, Jack."

Jack sat back down, his head spinning, regret and remorse washing over him like a tidal wave. He didn't dare use his usual argument of *"How do you expect us to afford this comfortable life if I don't work so hard?"* It would be a wasted effort, and Jack was all about efficiency. He was devastated. Even though he was rarely home, he loved his family, his wife. He needed them as a counterbalance to his overwhelming work life.

Darla grabbed her suitcase. He hadn't even noticed it sitting near the door. "We'll be at my mom's. My sister took the kids there after school. We'll miss you, but we just can't, I just can't do it anymore."

With that she was out the door. Jack's first instinct was to run after her and beg, but he knew his wife too well for that. This decision was well thought out, and it was final. No turning back.

Jack slumped on the couch and cried like he hadn't since he was a boy.

"That day was a whole nine months, two

weeks and four days ago. But who's counting," Jack said to Big Tony. He went on to regal him with the saga of his overworked life; his over-commitment to his job, his striving to be the best employee – ever. That's why he permitted – *permitted!* – his work to take precedence over his family.

"I guess the straw that broke the camel's back was when I missed Henry's birthday party one Saturday, like a coupla weeks before she left. I got called into work for some big presentations on Monday, and the blueprints weren't correct so they tagged me because I always say yes," said Jack.

Tony just listened and nodded, but Jack could see his face was getting red. After a second, Jack thought something might be medically wrong with him. "Tony, are you okay?" asked Jack.

"Yeah, sure, it's just that listening to your story, it brought back a rush of memories of my old job. Kinda bad memories," said Tony.

"Oh," said Jack with surprise, "I thought this was always your life. I mean, you seem to love it. It's just so you."

"Yeah, I love it, it's great. But I had another career, before."

"What did you do?"

"I was a bond trader on Wall Street for 12 years," said Tony with the smallest of smiles. Jack was shocked and a little impressed.

"Never figured you for a Wall Street wise guy," said Jack. "That's crazy."

"I know, looking back, it was a crazy, bad fit," he said and smiled. "But dude, I was really good at it. I made money like I was printing it. It almost wrecked me," said Tony.

"How?" asked Jack.

"Well, for one thing, it almost wrecked my family. The hours were long, the commute was longer, the pressure was enough to put you in an early grave. One day, my dear, sweet wife, she," Big Tony suddenly got teary, something Jack thought he'd never see from this barrel-chested guy who seemed to love life and everyone around him. Tony went on. "She gave me an ultimatum: it's the job, or me and the kids. Choose now." said Tony, wiping his eyes.

"If it wasn't for that, from that kind-heart-

ed woman. She saved my life and my family in one fell swoop. And as you can imagine, I chose them," said Tony.

"Wait, wait, saved your life? How did she save your life?"

"At 47, I'd already had a heart attack. Doc said it was from the constant stress. Not un-common in that line of work," said Tony.

"So you would have been dead if you kept it up?" asked Jack with real concern. He won-dered if his doctor might come to the same conclusion. If he ever actually saw the doctor, that is.

"Yeah, maybe, probably. I got this hardcore, second-generation immigrant work-ethic thing going on. You know what I'm talking about. *'Never give up'*, my dad used to say, *'no matter what kinda garbage they throw at you. No matter how tough, how grueling, how awful it gets, never give up. Never quit!'* said Big Tony.

This struck a major chord with Jack. Quit, the dreaded word that had plagued his life since he was 11.

"Never quit. Yeah, I heard it, too," said Jack.

"Shamed me with it, used like a blunt instrument on me from my stepfather to my coaches. Same thing. The same speech. *'You quit now, and you'll be a quitter the rest of your life!'*" said Jack.

Tony chuckled as he shook his head. "Yeah, if I had a buck for every time I heard that, I could retire to Aruba. You know what, Jack? It's all a mindgame," Jack smiled, feeling a sense of release.

"Your life, the Good Book says, is like a whisper, a blade of grass springing up today and burning off in the sun tomorrow," said Tony in a heartfelt voice. "So don't waste it trying to please everyone else. You gotta keep your family together, no matter what!" said Tony, punctuating that last word.

Jack nodded solemnly. Tony was right. Jack was torn between doing the right thing and the expected thing. They pulled hard against each other.

Jack walked to the parking lot. Tony came up beside him, put his hefty hand on his shoulder and simply said, "You can fix this, Jack. You can fix it. Do the right thing before it's

too late." Jack nodded. To his own surprise, he found himself doing something completely out of character. He hugged Big Tony. It wasn't out of character for Tony. He wrapped Jack in a bear hug, then kissed him on the top of his head. "You take care, and remember what Big Tony says. You can fix this."

Jack returned to his overworked life. Tony had one last burning question for Jack. "So, this is pretty random but, whoever came up with the saying, *the straw that broke the camel's back?* I've BEEN on a camel in Egypt. I can't imagine a single straw breaking their backs. Weird, huh?" Jack chuckled.

"Yeah, pretty weird," said Jack. He kept smiling as Tony returned to the deli. His friend had been good medicine. Jack left with a lighter load than when he arrived.

# CHAPTER 5

Back at work, Jack had a hard time concentrating. His work was piling up at the edge of his desk. After 4:00, Arthur rumbled by and noticed how little Jack had done.

"Jack, what's going on? I thought you worked on these over lunch. Aren't you about done?" asked Arthur.

"I'm not feeling well, I'm having a hard time concentrating," said Jack. Arthur was not listening.

"Those drawings don't look like they've been double-checked, and that's not like you," said Arthur.

"Yeah, I got distracted. I'll work on them now and get something to you in the morning," replied Jack.

"Not acceptable. We're presenting tomorrow! You know that. We have to have those drawings to win this project. I'm talking the bottom line here, I'm talking our bonuses and, should I go on?" Jack was flustered. He wanted to say yes, the way he always said yes, always toed the line. But his mind, body, and spirit were not doing well. Couldn't everyone see

that? Jack stumbled through his mental fog for a solution.

"Okay, uh, maybe if Freddy can help me? I'd finish tonight and have them on your desk first thing in the a.m.–"

"Not gonna happen," interrupted Arthur. "Freddy's kid has an important basketball game. They're in the finals!" Jack could feel something brimming up inside that he hadn't felt at work in years. It took a second for him to realize what it was. Anger. It was not pretty.

"Oh my God, Arthur, the finals! I didn't know. How uninformed of me," said Jack sarcastically. His smartass response took Arthur off guard. Where was the straight-shooting Jack he'd always known?

"What the heck?" said Arthur. "Why are you talking to me like this? You always say yes. You're our yes guy. That's, that's your thing. Plan to hunker down tonight." But Jack interrupted him, shaking his head. No, no, no.

"So you're saying that since my kids are with my estranged wife two and a half hours away, I have no life and Freddy does? His after-hours time is more precious than mine?"

Jack was barely able to control his simmering resentment. Arthur thought about it for a second before responding.

"I wouldn't put it quite that way but, yeah. Why bust his chops when you got nothing better to do? See you in the morning. With the drawings done," said Arthur flippantly as he walked away.

Jack was mad. Furious. He wanted to turn over some tables,no, better to kick some trash cans, really hard, because they don't hurt your foot but still make an impressive racket! As soon as he saw Arthur leave, his anger kicked into action. Jack walked out, leaving his work untouched.

Jack was in his car quickly. Without even realizing where he was going, he started driving east. Because that's where Darla and the kids were. He wanted to see them, hug them, just be with them, maybe even get a glimpse of his darling Darla. He missed her like the seashore missed the waves.

Jack was in such a haze that it took almost a half hour of driving before he realized he was heading towards Meadowridge, the town

where Darla's mom lived. He pulled over to the side of the road and stopped. Knowing he couldn't show up unannounced, he dialed Darla's cellphone. It rang and rang then kicked over to voicemail.

Jack hung up without leaving a message. All he wanted to do was see his kids, even if they were asleep and maybe, maybe tell Darla that he was starting to realize why she left. He thought about dialing again. But would that make it look like he was stalking her. He didn't call. He just dropped the car in gear and kept heading in that direction, anyway.

Jack missed Darla. He missed the kids, too, but, Darla most of all. He'd loved her from the moment they met, and he just felt incomplete without her at his side.

CHAPTER
6

They met in college. For Jack, college was not the traditional four-year institution covered in ivy with lots of drinking and backslapping camaraderie. It was more practical. It had to be, because his stepfather and mother couldn't afford to send him to one of those schools, or to any school for that matter.

"If you wanna go to college, fine, just don't expect us to pay for it," Leroy had said on several occasions. Maybe Leroy had forgotten that he'd already mentioned that little detail, over and over and over. Maybe his memory was fading from too much beer. Either way, it was like rubbing salt in his wounds. Nevertheless, Jack was determined to go, and he would not quit trying until he had his degree in civil engineering. He loved the inflexibility of math. It suited him.

Jack's work ethic was second to none, and all his teachers and professors noticed. He started at the local community college, lived at home, worked two part-time jobs, saved all his earnings, and was able to get his basic requirements done in two years. Of course, it meant summer school classes but he kept it light, only two per session. He saved enough to go to the local university, only eight miles from their home, and never once thoughts of getting an apartment or joining a frat or even going to a football game. Jack's focus was laser tight and singular: get that degree. The degree was the ticket to higher-paying jobs, living in a nicer home and all sorts of other benefits, such as making sure your kids didn't feel guilty if they asked for a new pair of shoes.

Jack was known for working harder than anyone, playing less than anyone, earning better grades than everyone. It was no surprise that he was set to graduate a semester early. When Jack's senior year rolled around and his school load lightened because he was so far ahead, he got to take a couple of "frivolous classes," as Leroy had labeled them. *Greek and Latin Influences on the English Language*, for instance. Jack was fascinated by all the English words and sayings that were derived from Greek, Latin and French. He got an A, as usual.

While Jack didn't have much time to socialize until he was a senior, he met a guy his sophomore year whom he could really call a friend. Charlie Dettinger. Charming Charlie, they called him. He was the total opposite of Jack but, for some reason, they really liked each other. He was a wisecracking, fun-loving guy from New York City whose father was a stockbroker. He must have made good money, because Charlie never had to work and spent money like it would never run out. (It did one day, but that's a completely different story.)

In the spring semester, Jack started working as a waiter at a diner near campus. Since he'd worked his entire way through college, holding down two and even three jobs at a time while cramming in as many classes as possible, this one was a piece of cake — or pie, as the Ridgeway Diner was famous for its pies. The shifts were only four hours long, and Jack made some decent tips. He had discovered that talking, smiling, and trying to enjoy your work was a lot better than the opposite. He was naturally shy, not wanting to be the center of attention, but waiting tables, along with hanging around Charlie, brought him out of his shell.

"Kind sir, where might I find an empty table?" said voice behind Jack as he helped the busboy clear a table. The bad British accent and affected voice told Jack instantly who it was.

"Well, my good man," replied Jack in an equally bad British accent, "there's nothing here for your ilk, so I suggest you bugger off." Jack smiled. Charlie sniffed the air for a second as if he was downwind of a hog farm, then burst out laughing.

"Your accent is terrible," said Jack.

"No worse than yours," said Charlie.

"Come on, I'll set you up. How many?"

"There will be three of us so." Charlie stopped when he saw a friend coming their way, smiling and waving. A curvy blonde with ruby red lips, just Charlie's type. Charlie introduced her as Jack led the way to a four-top.

"Well, it's nice to meet you, Linda. Let me," said Jack as he pulled out her chair.

"Such a gentleman, thanks," said Linda.

"Why don't you join us?" said Charlie. Jack chuckled at this typical question from a guy who led the life of a playboy.

"You see, I do this thing called 'work.' I know you're not familiar with it, but some of us have to," said Jack.

"Work, smirk, you have your whole life to do the grind."

"I know, but the tips are good, and I'd have to literally quit on the spot, right now to hang with you so…" replied Jack as he handed them their menus.

"Then do it. Just quit, my good man," said Charlie, half joking.

"It's not in my DNA."

"But you quit those other jobs, what were they again?

"I didn't quit anything, I was let go." Jack started to say, then faded off, uncomfortable with the subject.

"Because why?" asked Linda.

"Because he was working three jobs, taking 18 units, and was falling asleep at in class, right?" asked Charlie.

"Right, right, I was let go. But I didn't quit. I never quit. I persevere. It's like my mantra, or my middle name," said Jack, getting back into the rhythm of their constant ribbing.

"That's a weird middle name," said a voice behind them. A lovely voice, soothing but direct and confident. A wide smile broke across Charlie's face. Jack turned and saw her. He was suddenly at a loss for words. No witty comebacks, just one of those jaw-dropping *"I think I met the one"* kind of moments. Her name was Darla.

CHAPTER 7

Jack, stupefied, truly could not find a single word. He could not think of *anything* to say this to this dark-haired, honey-voiced, lovely woman. The green sweater casually tied around her neck, as was the fashion in those days, made her green eyes all the more intense as she smiled politely at Jack. He pulled out her chair without a hitch, but his nerves were raw and his body tense. So raw that he thought he'd better take a break in the kitchen to calm down before he broke something.

He was sure he'd made a bit of a fool of himself. He might as well have drooled on himself! Anyone with eyes could see he had been immediately smitten with Darla. But she was polite and gracious and pretended not to notice. Charlie noticed, though, and had to keep himself from laughing out loud. He'd never seen Jack react to any other woman like he did to Darla.

Darla had a mysterious effect on Jack He remembered his very first crush in eighth grade. Her name was Ginger, with locks of curly red hair, freckles, and a crooked smile that made him tongue-tied. He soon got over her, once Ginger's true self reared its ugly head when she bullied his stepsister Olivia at recess one day. This was different, though. It wasn't just a rush of random teen hormones, but rather a feeling that he could conquer the world if he had Darla by his side.

Jack removed himself to the back on the diner, just off the kitchen, where his co-workers took quick breaks. He was practicing his deep breathing exercises when his manager walked by, then stopped, a scowl on his sweaty brow.

"Hey champ. Why aren't you working? It's only a four-hour shift for cryin' out loud! Get back on the floor!" Off Jack went, really wishing now that he'd done what Charlie suggested and quit. But he couldn't quit. That was just part of who he was.

Back on the floor, he served one table, re-filled the water glasses of another and walked over to Charlie, Linda, and Darla. He fought to keep his nerves under control.

"You guys ready to order?" said Jack.

"What do you recommend?" asked Darla.

"The food. The paper napkins are under-cooked, and the silverware has a metallic taste," replied Jack. They all laughed. Darla turned to Charlie.

"You didn't tell me he was funny, too."

"That's because I didn't know. I guess you girls bring out the comedian in him," said Charlie without looking up from the menu.

"Actually it's more."Jack said, searching for the right word," smartassery. I learned from the best." Charlie had to chuckle in spite of Jack upstaging him.

"You're welcome. In return, I'd like my meal on the house, please," said Charlie.

"Actually I'm gonna charge you double," replied Jack. Darla interrupted, setting down her menu.

"So how did you two meet?" she asked. Before Jack could reply, Charlie casually cut in. "Sophomore year. We both signed up for the same club."

"Which one?" asked Darla.

"The Future Dictators of America."

"Yeah, every other member was bald and

had a monocle," said Jack.

"We hit it off right away because we knew by joining forces we could actually achieve world domination," said Charlie.

"The best of pals," replied Jack.

"You two should take your comedy routine on the road," said Linda.

"I agree," said Darla.

"Yeah but if we did, who would be here to serve you our mediocre burgers and under-cooked fries?" said Jack.

"Like I said," Charlie said, patting the extra seat at the four-top, "come join us, leave your apron, and hang with us." Jack wanted to so badly he could feel his mouth go dry, but his sense of responsibility took over. That's when it hit him – *this was a setup!* Charlie was trying to set him up with Darla, and man, he had done good! It took all the willpower Jack could muster to refuse. What if he offered an alternative.

"I just can't, but how about I meet you guys later? My shift is over at 9:00," said Jack. Charlie nodded.

"Okay, we'll be at *The Tumbler*, having a beer and shooting some nine-ball," replied Charlie.

"I'll be there soon as I can. Now, what can I get you?" asked Jack in his most businesslike tone.

"The world, my friend, the world, because you owe me," said Charlie, covering his mouth with the menu on the last few words. But Darla heard it anyway. Jack glanced over at her. She blushed and smiled as she handed him the menu. Jack could feel himself blushing, too, but he didn't care.

"Cheeseburger, no onions, crispy fries, and nothing undercooked please," said Darla.

"Excellent choice, my kind of girl," said Jack, louder than he had intended. Darla blushed even more, and they all started to laugh.

When his shift ended, Jack was headed for the door in a flash, ready to change his shirt in his rusted-out Ford Escort. But just as he was about to clear the door, his manager grabbed him by the sleeve.

"Not so fast, Jack."

"What? My shift's over, and I'm meeting this beautiful girl who–"

"I don't care if you're meeting Elizabeth Taylor! You gotta clean your station. The busboy went home sick, and it's your responsibility," said the killjoy.

"I never have–" Jack began to say, but the manager cut him off again.

"No buts, it's part of the job." And with that, the manager turned back toward his office.

"I quit!" shouted Jack with such overt emotion that the manager stopped in his tracks. A slow grin broke across his face as he turned back.

"No, you won't. It's just who you are, Jack." He walked off. Steaming and frustrated, Jack paused, caught between his desires and his duty. He obeyed begrudgingly. The manager was right. The busboy-waiter code called for him to clean his station. He was finished in about thirty minutes. Thirty precious minutes that he could have been spending with the delightful, charming, beautiful, and interested in him for some reason, Darla.

Jack drove a bit too fast and almost sideswiped a car turning right in his haste to get to the club, but he quickly found a parking place close to the front door. It was a Thursday night, and the place was jumping. Weekends were even more crowded, but the party-hearties at the college started their weekends on Thursday, when happy lasted till 9:00. It was 9:20 as he crossed the threshold and started scanning the crowd for Charlie, Linda and Darla. He spotted Darla right away.

"Hey, you made it!" she said and gave him a quick hug.

"Yeah, are you leaving already?" he replied with disappointment.

Darla looked disappointed, too, as she replied, "I have a final that counts for half my grade tomorrow, and I have to finish studying and get some sleep." Was she sincere or just being polite? Jack couldn't tell.

"Well, I hope I run into you again sometime soon," he said, trying to keep his own discouragement from showing.

"Me too. How about Saturday night? I could run into you at my front door, and we

could run into each other for, oh, I don't know, a couple of hours or so that evening?" Darla said with a smile. Jack was taken aback. He'd never known a young woman to be so bold. He would come to find out that Darla was not only captivating and beautiful but direct. Very direct.

"I could manage to run into you then, at, say, 7:30?"

"Good, see ya then, and bring flowers," she said while starting to walk off.

"Okay but, why?" he asked, perplexed at such a request.

"Because I like them, and they're nice." With that, Darla was gone. Jack stood there like a dope. At least he felt like a dope, staring after Darla, hoping for one last glimpse as she reached her car. He could barely see her. He thought she smiled and gave him a quick wave. He waved back. And this time, he was truly a dope —because it wasn't Darla he was waving at, just some random person who may or may not have even been a woman.

CHAPTER
8

C oming into Meadowridge, Jack had no idea what he would do when he actually got to the house. His mother-in-law, Carla, probably wouldn't even let him in at this late hour. And who could blame her? It was about 9:00 when he arrived at the place where Darla and the kids where now living. So all he could do after this two hour, forty-five minute drive was sit and stare at the house.

Jack was nervous. What if a cautious neighbor mistook him for a stalker hanging around the house? He calmed himself. Most of the neighbors had to know his car by now, since he'd visited several times. Actually, he'd seen the kids more in the last nine months than in the past 4 years combined, sadly. It had been almost four weeks since he'd visited them last. He'd been working weekends because Arthur had decided that since Jack had no life, why not abuse him even more? A vision swam through Jack's mind of Arthur as one of those cartoon fat-cat bosses with an unlit cigar dangling from his of greasy lips.

As he sat in front of the house, Jack's resentment started to turn into anger, even rage. He hadn't felt like this since the first time he

was tagged as a quitter. He fought the emotion down. He wouldn't let Arthur get the best of his emotions. Jack shook his head violently to get the image of fat-cat Arthur out of his head and focus on the moment at hand. He was here to see his kids. He glued his eyes on the home's bay windows. But he couldn't see inside. He got out and walked down their sidewalk, trying to look as nonchalant as possible.

Jack could see Harry at the dining room table, doing some homework. From Harry's posture, Jack could tell it must be math, again. His kids hadn't inherited Jack's math proficiency was not something either of his kids inherited from him. They were more creative, given to spontaneous performances of songs, drawings, and stories. They took after Darla in that way. At one time, she had considered being a playwright, but life and kids got in the way. She was really good, though, writing two plays that their college drama department staged to glowing reviews. Jack remembered being very proud of her. He thought she had a real gift. He always reminded her that theater was a very tough, capricious way to make a living. He had warned her to think of it only as a hobby. Darla had been unhappy about that. Jack's work ethic and common sense won the day. Darla listened to him and never really pursued her dream.

Just then, Jack heard someone coming down the sidewalk.

"Jack?" said the man's voice. Jack turned to see their neighbor Russell, a kind, older man walking his golden retriever, Bessie, carrying a plastic bag filled with Bessie's poop.

"Oh hi, Russell. Lovely evening, isn't it?" said Jack, embarrassed and trying to cover it.

"It is. So…" Russell hesitated, "… late to the party?" He glanced at the house where Jack's estranged wife and kids lived.

"Yeah, I was supposed to be here earlier, but I got caught up at work," said Jack, shoving his hands into his pockets nervously. Russell nodded and waited for a moment before responding.

"Common story with men your age, I suppose," said Russell.

"Unfortunately, yes." Jack was growing more comfortable these days with silence, the art of shutting up, not feeling the urgent need to fill any conversation gap with useless words.

Russell didn't seem interested in small talk, either. He responded, "Well, they're good kids. I know they miss you. 'Night."

"Thanks, good night Russell," replied Jack. He stood there awkwardly as Russell walked off. Clearly this poorly thought-out act of courage was not going to pay off. But as he returned to his late model 3-series BMW, he had a brilliant idea. "I'll just stick around and see them tomorrow," he thought to himself. I'll call in sick, just like every other slacker I've had to cover for."

He whipped out his phone. But instead of calling work, he decided to text Darla. She always let it go to voicemail when he phoned. He assumed she just didn't want to talk to him, and he was right. A text would always get through to her.

The text was a simple, white lie: *I'm doing some work in the area tomorrow and was wondering if it would be okay for me to pick up the kids after school. Cool with you?* He sent it and waited till he saw the ellipses at the bottom on the text. Yes! She'd seen it, and was probably, hopefully, going to respond. His patience paid off as Darla's text came through: *I don't see why not. I'll make sure the school has you on the pickup list.*

Jack almost got a rash when telling a fib, so he was over the moon at the success of his little white lie. Yes, it wasn't true. He was trying to salvage what was left of a relationship with his own kids. And that made everything worth it. Pleased with himself, Jack drove off to find a cheap motel, a toothbrush, and some food.

CHAPTER
9

Jack woke up early, ready to get out of the rather seedy motel he'd ended up in. He'd had to sleep on top of the bedspread because, after pulling back the covers, it was obvious the sheets had not been washed. It looked as if the bathroom hadn't been thoroughly cleaned in several days. After a restless night, he could have sworn he'd been eaten alive by bedbugs. He just wanted a place to crash for six or seven hours, and he'd made it through the night.

Out and about in the crisp fall air, Jack's first order of business was to get some walking shoes and exercise clothes. Last time he had found the time to exercise, Darla had purchased him some Spandex shorts so they could ride bikes on the one beach vacation they had taken before Harry was born. Jack thought no grown man should have to suffer wearing bike shorts, so as soon as they returned home, he had buried them in a random drawer and hoped Darla would forgot about them.

After finding a Target, Jack got his clothes and was off to find a nice trail. He liked walking or hiking, because he could think, meditate, pray, and get some cardio at the same time.

Win-win. As soon as he found a lovely park with a three-mile walk around the perimeter of the park and into some woods, that's when his phone started buzzing.

Jack had already left a message with HR to say he was taking a personal day. However, that didn't stop Arthur from harassing him. The phone rang nonstop for about five minutes, one call after another. Arthur clearly wasn't satisfied with leaving a message. Instead, he just called and called, expecting Jack to pick up.

Jack refused. He left the annoying thing in the car. He knew what Arthur would say. A dress down. Lots of histrionics about how he'd let down the team. They'd probably lose the bid. What the hell where you thinking!? Yada yada yada. The same manipulative song and dance. Oh, and shaming. Lots of shaming. Arthur's classic whine: "You did this on purpose, didn't you?!"

Jack started to think about playing the long game. He decided he should keep all Arthur's messages, as evidence of a sort. He was thinking of himself, his future, and his family. Not the good of the company. Not Arthur's performance bonuses. The very thought was empowering. Yes, it came coupled with a twinge of guilt, but Jack pushed through it, focusing on taking his brisk walk on this beautiful fall day.

The hours until pickup time went slowly. Jack found the one movie theater in town that had not closed after the great Covid-19 readjustment. But the film he thought he might like turned out to be a depressing, dystopian movie about some kids all so predictable he fell asleep. That restless night had done a number on him.

At 2:45, he headed to school to get the kids. He was pretty excited. The school kids came bursting forth not 20 seconds after the end-of-day bell. Happy, joyous, free. The sort of joy that only comes from children who haven't become. Jack couldn't help but smile when he saw his own kids. Harry and Heather ran towards him with reckless abandon, so fast he worried they might fall. They hugged him hard around the waist. He wanted to bend down and kiss them over and over, but he didn't wan to embarrass them.

"How're my kiddos? Man, it's good to see you, both of you!" said Jack. Tears welled up.

"We're great, daddy!" said Heather, the wis-

est first grader alive, at least he thought so. She was full of kindness and empathy and maturity, all of which she had gotten from her mom. Harry was more circumspect, quiet and a bit shy, like Jack at his age. But the kids seemed, to love him as did his teachers. Except when it came to math.

"Dad, we're really glad to see you. I could really use your help on the whole math thing," said Harry, trying to appear cool.

"Yeah, that's a tough subject for you, huh?" said Jack.

"Math sucks!" said Harry.

"Excuse me, but when did you start using that kind of language?" asked Jack.

"Ever since he staring hanging out with Oscar, he has a potty mouth," said Heather.

"No, he does not have a potty mouth, tattletale! He's just... colorful!" said Harry defensively. Jack had to smile.

"Well, maybe we just color inside the lines when it comes to language. I know your mom and grandmother would appreciate that," said Jack softly as he started ushering them towards his car.

"Okay. So…" said Harry, brightening, "where are we going!?"

"Some place fun!? Remember that place with the popcorn and games and warm cookies, daddy?" asked Heather.

"Buzzers!" shouted Harry with a fist pump.

"I do remember! And I thought we'd go there again but only, and I mean only, if you don't beg for seconds because you won't eat your dinner and that would be–"

"Bad!" Harry and Heather said together.

"Yeah, your mom and grandma are still mad at me for that, but let's go!" said Jack. And off they went.

Jack was smart enough to let Darla know that he was taking the kids to Buzzer's. He promised they'd each have only one popcorn and a single warm chocolate chip cookie. Just as something to do in between the awesome arcade games, of course.

When they finished up around 5:30, Jack decided to pick up a few extra cookies for Darla and her mom. They might warm Darla's heart a little, he thought or hoped.

Sadly, he had misread the situation. When they reached the door, Darla opened it hard and fast, hustling the kids inside. Jack offered her the cookies. "Here, I got some extra for you," he said, holding them out.

Darla shook her head and blocked his way in. "Don't think you can sweet talk, or sweet treat, your way back into our good graces. You had your chance, and you blew it." With that, she shut the door in his face.

Jack wasn't the only one taken aback. Standing right behind Darla, her mother scowled, arms crossed, at the exchange.

"That was rude," said Carla.

"What'd you expect me to do, encourage him?" replied Darla sharply.

"I expect you to be kind to another human being, especially the father of your children. I expect you to give him the benefit of the doubt. Maybe he was just being thoughtful."

"He should have been thoughtful years ago. He should have quit that stupid job and taken a less demanding one so he could spend time with the people he claimed to love." Darla walked past her mom. Carla didn't move or react. She just sighed and went to set the table while the kids washed up.

Jack drove home, filled with mixed emotions. Grateful for the uninterrupted time with this kids but feeling kicked in the sternum by Darla's harsh words. He could only breathe deep and hope for better days.

CHAPTER 10

Jack returned to work the following day. Within no less than three minutes, Arthur came to his office wearing his usual ugly striped tie and a foreboding look on his thick brow.

"I need to see you in my office. Now," he said, smacking the door with his fist and walking off. Jack slowly stood and followed. His heart started to pick up speed, but he forced himself to breathe and slow it down. As he walked by Michael, Jack shrugged with an *I'm in trouble now'* gesture, just like the one time he was called to the principal's office in grade school. Michael crossed himself and made the universal sign of *I'll pray for you.*

Jack steeled himself as he followed Arthur. Maybe, just maybe, he might have an ace up his sleeve.

Arthur's voluminous office was filled with trophies from his kid's athletic endeavors and framed pictures of him with various dignitaries. He was particularly proud of his photo with Bill Clinton. They were both smiling, probably caught in the aftermath of a good joke and no doubt a cocktail or two.

Entering the intimidating room, Jack was surprised to see the HR maven, Ms. Schneider, the most intimidating woman he'd ever met. No one messed with Ms. Schneider, especially upper management. She had called many upper management people onto the proverbial carpet and wasn't afraid to stand up for the underlings. She could be harsh, even cruel, but Jack knew that she was fair.

"Hello, Jack," said Ms. Schneider.

"So it's one of those kind of meetings?" replied Jack.

"How do you mean that?" she asked.

"Let's dispense with the small talk and get to business. I'm a busy man!" said Arthur, as if he was in charge of this meeting. But Ms. Schneider shot him a look that could stop a bear cold in his tracks.

"We're all busy, Arthur." She turned back to Jack. "Again, how do you mean that?"

"I only meant that whenever HR is involved, it's pretty serious," replied Jack. Ms. Schneider chewed on his answer for a few seconds. Her deliberate thoughtfulness didn't bother Jack, but he could see Arthur getting more and more agitated. *Good,* he thought, *he'll blow his stack here in a minute and show his true colors.*

But he didn't. This sort of intervention made him angry, since he preferred to dole out punishment and rewards as he saw fit. Ms. Schneider, however, was the queen and she spoke with authority. Arthur may have been a blustering asshole and a heavy-handed, but he was also smart. He kept his mouth shut.

"I'm not here to make any snap judgments. I just want to find out what's going on and address any issues," Ms. Schneider said. That was only partially true, to be honest. Arthur had probably complained so loudly yesterday that word had gotten back to her.

"Why don't you tell me what happened yesterday towards the end of the day?"

"Sure. I can tell you word for word what was said," responded Jack. Now Arthur rolled his eyes and let out a groan. But Ms. Schneider gave him another withering look, and he held up his hands in surrender.

Jack told his tale.

"As you know, my wife and I are estranged. She took the kids, and they live two and a half hours away. I missed my kids. I needed to see them. I was going to leave at a reasonable hour when Arthur came in and said I'd have to stay and fix some drawings for the Fort Johnson Bridge project."

Jack took a deep breath and went on, "Arthur said I'd have to stay and finish them since the meeting was set for the next morning. I suggested that if a colleague helped me, we could finish quickly. Arthur replied, and I quote, 'Not gonna happen, his kid has an important basketball game. They're in the finals!' And I said, 'You're saying that since my kids are with my estranged wife, two and a half hours away, that I have no life and he does? That his after hours time is more precious than mine?'" Ms. Schneider seemed to clench her jaw, as if keeping it from falling open in shock.

Arthur couldn't take it anymore. "You're an exempt employee, so whining about overtime doesn't cut it. We all work extra hours so no…" But Ms. Schneider cut him off. "Let him finish."

Arthur, turning red with rage, slumped

back in his chair.

Turning to Jack, Ms. Schneider asked, "What was said next?"

Jack picked up his story. "Arthur said, 'Yes. Why bust his chops when you got nothing better to do?' and then he left my office," said Jack. A tense silence filled the room as Ms. Schneider wrote notes. Jack filled the silence by pointing out: "Might I add, in the last seven years, I have only missed three days of work. Once, when my boy broke his arm and his mother was out of town. Once when I was hurling up my guts from the stomach flu. And yesterday because I was feeling ill and could not concentrate on my work," said Jack.

"Bull crap! You were willfully derelict in your duties. If it was up to me, I'd fire your ass right here and now!" shouted Arthur.

He'd crossed a line. "Do not say another word, Arthur" she snapped. She took a moment to calm herself as she look at Jack intently.

"Jack, going over your records, I can see you haven't taken a real vacation in a long, long time," she said.

"In the last five years, I haven't taken anything more than a couple of long weekends. I've worked plenty of Saturdays. I even missed my son's birthday party to get a project done. I destroyed my marriage by being loyal to this company. Why? Because I do not quit." he said, his voice quivering with passion. Ms. Schneider took a deep breath.

"Jack, I think you need to take some time off. I suggest two weeks. Starting immediately."

Arthur leapt from his chair. "Two weeks!? No way! He's gotta finish this project or we're—" Ms. Schneider had had enough. She jabbed a finger at Arthur.

"Sit. Down." she said, unabashed anger flowing through her voice. Arthur slowly sat back down, but like a petulant kid whose very manner shouts defiance. Watching him, Jack could almost hear what Arthur would say to the CEO about Ms. Schneider. She didn't care.

Ms. Schneider turned calmly to Jack. "I see that you've accumulated lots of paid vacation time, sick days, and personal days, so if you need more than two weeks, just shoot me an email." She stood with a smile, extending her hand.

"Thanks," said Jack, then, pointedly, "It's nice to be valued."

"You are a very important employee, integral to this team. Would you mind shutting the door on your way out?" Ms. Schneider turned to face Arthur, who suddenly looked a little green around the gills. Jack managed to keep the broad smile from breaking across his face until he had closed the door behind him.

"So, bro, what went down? What the hell made the old man so mad?" asked Michael, approaching anxiously.

"You free for lunch? I'm buying," said Jack.

"A skinflint like you offering to buy lunch? I'd be a fool to turn that down. I want to hear everything," Michael said, fist bumping Jack..

"Cool, fool, let's do it," said Jack. He began to hum a happy tune as they left the office.

CHAPTER
11

Driving over to Big Tony's, Jack had a few minutes to think. Of course, Darla and the kids immediately came to mind. But for the first time, he could now see that there might – *might!* – be some light at the end of the tunnel. Even, perhaps, a way to get his family back together. ack was not the kind of guy who expected good things would just happen to him. *You have to go out and make your own way,* Jack thought. Hard work, dedication, never giving up no matter what were the defining characteristics that shaped his life. Ge began to wonder, did they cost him his wife?

Jack was thrust into the memory of their first date. Those daisies that his mom talked him into buying. Their only scent was the generic smell of a plant. He'd wanted to bring roses. His mom said roses made too bold a statement. He regretted taking her advice as soon as he rang Darla's doorbell. He remembered being nervous but trying to hide it. He tried being clever or funny to cover his nerves. Sometimes that worked, and sometimes it didn't. He remembered hoping that he could split the difference between being a smartass and just a guy with a good sense of humor.

When Darla answered the door, all Jack's best intentions flew out the window. His jaw dropped at her beauty. She had her hair in an updo, exposing her long, elegant neck, and she was wearing a loose sweater than hung low enough to expose just a little cleavage. Along with that, she wore boyfriend jeans and blue Converse tennis shoes. Even though she looked as down-to-earth as you can get, to Jack, she looked ready for a glass slipper.

"Oh hey, right on time, and, daisies?" Darla said, taking the small bouquet wrapped in clear cellophane, finished with a small white bow.

"How did you know they were my favorites?" she said with a gentle smile.

"Wild guess," said Jack. Those were about the only words he could get out. No girl, no woman rather, had ever had this effect on him. Her roommates were there, but they barely looked up when she introduced him. It turned out, she had so many suitors, this was just another Saturday night.

Later that night, over dinner at an upscale pizza place, they shared a modestly priced bottle of Cabernet. Everything was picture perfect

up to that point. Lots of smiles, laughter, stories, good food. The wine had a kick. Too much
of a kick, as it turned out, for Darla. After her
first glass, she started making strange faces.

"Are you okay?" Jack asked. "You look like
you're not feeling well."

"No, yeah, I mean, yeah, I suddenly feel
rotten. Almost like," she said, as her face started
to turn red. "Can we get out of here?"

Jack grabbed her hand, dropped a wad of
cash on the table, and led Darla out the door.
Just in time. As Jack opened the car door, Darla vomited all over his shoes, his 'special occa-
sion' loafers, no less. His concern for his shoes
quickly took a distant second to helping Darla.
He felt a twinge of guilt to think he might be
responsible for all this.

"Let's get you home," he said, pulling out
some napkins from the glove box. Darla wiped
her mouth, tears welling up.

"I'm so sorry I ruined our first date. I wanted it to be so special and…" Darla choked off
her words as she prepared to hurl again.

"Nonsense! You did nothing wrong." Darla vomited again and again. Jack did the only thing he could think of: hold her hair back, as half of it had fallen out of her updo.

After she finished, Jack wiped her mouth and drove her home, slowly, her window down on this cool, spring night. They found out later she was allergic to the tannins in red wine.

They laughed about it for years, but that moment anchored their relationship for a long time to come. Jack was kind and gentle in a tense situation. It was a trait he had learned from his mother, and Darla found it endearing.

Jack met Michael at the deli counter, where they both ordered the meatball sub. Michael couldn't wait to ask.

"So, what went down in the meeting with Arthur and the HR lady?"

"Arthur got a smackdown," said Jack with a slight grin.

"Oh my god, what? Tell me, what?" asked Michael.

"I don't want to go into details, but I have finally had enough of staying late, working weekends, and being the department whipping boy," said Jack. Michael was stunned.

"That's how you see yourself?"

"Yeah. What else would you call it?" "Oh, I don't know. Perhaps the hardest-working, most diligent guy we've all ever known," said Michael.

"Thanks for the vote of confidence," Jack replied. But he wasn't really comfortable with this unexpected praise. He'd had so little of it in his entire life, he didn't know how to respond to it. So he changed the subject.

"Uh, so, you wanna know the outcome of this fateful meeting?"

Michael nodded, digging into his meatball sub. "It started with Arthur berating me for not coming to the rescue for the team, again. But it ended with me being forced, forced, I tell you, to take a two-week vacation. Immediately. Maybe longer," said Jack. Michael almost choked on his sandwich.

"You taking a vacation is kinda like a polar bear with golf clubs. The two just don't fit," said Michael.

"I know. I usually get bored after a day or

two. I thought I'd put the time into something productive," said Jack with a wink.

"Did you just wink at me, or do you have something in your eye?"

"No, I winked. I've got something up my sleeve," said Jack with another wink.

"Okay, this is getting weird. Just tell me, and stop with the *wink wink nudge nudge* stuff," said Michael emphatically.

"I want to take a couple of classes and do some research on a new career path," said Jack, waiting for Michael's approval. But Michael crinkled his nose and pulled back with a look of shock.

"Dude, you're like forty-something! Don't ya think it's a little late to be starting over?" said Michael. Before Jack could even respond, though, a booming voice said, "Absolutely not!"

CHAPTER
12

B ig Tony, cleaning a nearby table, looked Michael in the eye as he plopped down in the seat across from him.

"Sorry, but I couldn't help but overhear. No offense, but that just is not true," said Tony, "I started over from scratch when I was getting close to fifty, and I have not one single regret," said Tony. Michael looked at him sideways.

"So what did you used to do?" asked Michael.

"I was an accountant for a while, then became a bond trader and lasted twelve whole years without dying on the floor," said Tony.

"There was that one heart-attack," said Jack.

"That was a wake-up call. I made some good money but, at what price glory, hey?" said Tony as he turned to Jack. "You, go explore, find out what you really wanna do and you won't stress so much."

"But, but," Michael started to say, looking a little panicked, "That would mean you've have to, you know, the Q word?" He stared at Jack, as if waiting for some dramatic response.

"The Q'word. What's that?" asked Jack.

"Quit. You'd have to quit!" Michael said loudly.

Hearing the word, a bead of sweat formed on Jack's upper lip. "Yes, I am well aware that if I find another passion, I'd have to, yes, quit," he replied. "Yes, that would be hard because, because I have always felt like I wasn't good enough or savvy enough or ambitious enough to do something on my own. This job gave me purpose. Yes, at times, it has also overwhelmed me. I go home at night and cannot stop thinking about it. I'm still at work in my head all night long, all weekend long. That's why I lost my wife, and my kids are, well, I don't even really know them," said Jack. He took a deep breath. "I know it's risky, scary even to think of quitting a good-paying job, and I'm not saying that I am, you know, um, quitting! But you only got one life to live so, maybe."

Michael interrupted, very serious. "You can't quit, dude. Our department will fall apart without you."

"I bet you guys could make do," said Tony, standing to leave.

"No! You don't understand, he's our go-to guy," Michael anxiously replied.

"You mean I'm the guy everyone goes to when they have to go somewhere else. I get to stay," said Jack. Michael couldn't argue. If he was honest, he had taken advantage of Jack's *never quit until the job's done* attitude more than a few times. Tony looked at Michael and shook his head.

"Geez, get a grip, man," said Tony as he went back to work.

"I'm sorry, Jack. I just can't stand the thought of you not being there. Look, if you do go off and, you know, start another civil engineering firm, once you get some funding, then please… hire me," said Michael with an exaggerated smile, trying to make light of his overreaction.

"If I do get up the nerve to leave, it will not be for another engineering firm," Jack replied.

"Then what? What do you know as well as civil engineering?"

"Nothing. But I want to find some options, some things to think about," said Jack.

He stood. "Let's go. I have a rough afternoon ahead of me. Gotta send a couple of emails to let people know I'm hitting the road for two whole weeks!"

Michael followed Jack out to the parking lot, hot on his heels. "You can't quit. I mean, you said it yourself. It's against your core values, your, your nature!"

"If you're quitting one thing to do another thing, is it really quitting? Besides, I want to take some time and evaluate my life, my priorities. And remember, my wife left me because I was—"

Michael couldn't stand it and interrupted. "You can't blame everything on that for the rest of your life," he blurted out.

Jack was miffed. Pissed off, even. Michael might be his best work friend, but he was crossing a line. "Look. I made choices, some good and some I regret. There's a time in everyone's life, when choices are made for you."

Michael was confused. "What exactly does that mean?"

Jack shook his head. He wasn't really sure

himself. But he forced himself to calm down. "Look. All I'm asking from you, and from all the people in my life, from everyone at work, is to let me take some time to think about what I want to do, instead of just doing what everyone expects me to do."

Michael chewed on that for a moment, then replied; "Okay. Do what you gotta do."

Back at work, Jack was true to his word. He typed out a couple of quick emails to his clients on his most pressing projects. His memos said, "I am going to be out of the office for two weeks for some personal time," and they told his clients whom they should contact if they had any questions. He wanted to type in a massive truth about how he'd taken very little time off in years and years, but thought better of it. He knew how gossip and rampant speculation could spread through an office and lead to all sorts of trouble, and he didn't want a lot of chatter among his clients and colleagues. Once he'd hit "Send" on the emails, he grabbed his satchel. He was out the door only a few minutes after returning from lunch.

Jack made it to the elevator bank and pressed the down button without having to ex-

plain to anyone where he was going or what was he thinking. The doors opened and he got on and pressed the ground floor button. But just as the door was about to close, an arm stuck in and stopped the whole process. Jack had a queasy feeling that this was not good. He was right. Not to his surprise, Arthur stepped into the elevator with him.

At first Arthur didn't even acknowledge Jack's presence which made Jack feel even queasier. As the elevator was about to reach the ground floor, he turned to Jack.

"I know what you're doing," said Arthur. Jack couldn't help but think about Coach Jessup all those years ago, as Arthur had virtually the identical tone and facial expression. "And it's not going to end well for you."

"What is it you think I'm doing, besides taking some well-deserved time off?" asked Jack. He knew this was not about vacation time. It was about having the stones to actually challenge his manager.

Arthur said nothing. But as the doors opened, he blocked Jack from getting off. As Jack tried to maneuver around him, Arthur grabbed his arm.

"Don't play me for a fool. I've let many a twerp like you go in my career and have no problem doing it again," he said. Jack gently removed his arm from Arthur's grasp.

"I am taking some time off to get my life back together. If you have an issue with that, take it up with Ms. Schneider. See ya in two weeks," said Jack. He went off whistling. He was not a good whistler, so he shifted to humming instead. The message couldn't have been clearer.

CHAPTER
13

Darla and her mother were preparing dinner in the kitchen. The kids were done with homework after only being told to get back to work twice (a new record).

"Is that ready for the oven?" asked Darla, as her mother put the last touches on a creamed chicken casserole.

"Yes. Is the oven on?" asked Carla.

"Indeed," Darla replied. Her mom slid the Pyrex dish inside and set the timer. Just then, Darla's phone pinged. She looked down at the text. Her face turned sour, and she sighed.

"What is it? Is something wrong?" asked Carla.

"It's Jack. He says he has some news and wants to talk to me," said Darla. She set her phone aside. Her mother looked at her, hands firmly planted on her hips.

"Well?" asked Carla.

"Well, what?" replied Darla, knowing full well what she meant.

"Are you going to respond to the man, the father of your children? Or not?"

"Why do you always have to remind me he's the kids' father? It's not like I've forgotten," Darla spat out.

"You owe him a certain level of courtesy, that's all."

"This 'big news' is most likely about him getting that promotion he's always wanted. After all, now that we're out of the picture, he can work even longer and harder for them," said Darla, not trying to hide her spite, "He's so enamored with that company he probably has a nice little cot in the corner of his office so he never has to leave."

"Would you stop!" spouted Carla. "The man may have worked too hard and neglected his family, I'll give you that. But in my generation, when you found a good job, you put in the extra hours without question and worked your fanny off. Once you had a good job, you never let it go. My parents were raised in the Depression—" Darla cut her off.

"Not the Depression story again, please. I know, I know, I know. But the Depression was almost 100 years ago. I wanted a husband who would be his own man, stand up to them. If they wouldn't respect any of his boundaries, he would find a company that would! That's all I'm saying and all I wanted." A long pause. Carla finally broke the silence.

"You don't know what's actually going on unless you talk to him," said Carla. Darla took another deep breath. She hated to admit it, but she had to follow her mom's advice.

"Okay, you're right," she said. She texted Jack back: *Fine. When do you want to chat?*

Jack rang her up later that day. The conversation was awkward, as Darla really didn't want to talk to him. Jack found her unnatural, frosty tone chilling. This was not the Darla he remembered.

"I'll come up and take the kids for a weekend trip. I'll check out some fun places and call you back, of course, to see if you approve," he said.

"Fine," she replied.

"I wanted you to know that I'm taking two full weeks off. With absolutely no contact from Arthur or anyone on the team, as prescribed by our tough-as-nails head of HR," said Jack in a

cheery tone. There was only silence on the other end. Had the line gone dead? Jack wondered.

Darla said nothing because Jack's words stirred some deep emotions in her, taking her to the verge of tears. She wanted to scream, *Why didn't you do that before this?! Why didn't you take time to take us all on a vacation?! That's the very least you could have done!"*

"Uh, hello? Are you still there?" he finally asked.

"Yeah, look, that's great, enjoy your time off. I gotta go."

"Wait. There's something else I wanted to tell you," he said.

"I gotta go," she replied, anxious to hang up before she broke down.

"It'll only take a second. I just wanted you to know that I'm taking time to, uh, explore some other, well, how do I put this, other careers? I just can't keep working like this. There must be better ways to make a living," he said. The positive response he hoped for did not come.

"Sounds good, talk to you later," Darla said

and hung up. She had to get off the phone before she cried, grieving once again the death of what had been a good and beautiful marriage.

Carla walked back into the room, immediately concerned. "What happened? Are you all right? Is Jack all right?" she asked.

"Yes, he's all right, he's just, he's taking two weeks off to get his act together, which, I don't know, makes me happy for him but sad for us," she said with a touch of sarcasm.

"Darla, maybe he will. Maybe he will," said Carla, hugging her daughter.

"Or maybe it just falls into the too-little-too-late category," replied Darla, squirming out of her mother's hub. But Carla just shook her head.

"It's never too late. Never. Go take a moment. I'll make sure the kids help set the table and wash up."

"Thanks, Mom," Darla replied.

CHAPTER
14

By his third day of being off, Jack was already starting to get restless. He was a doer. He didn't like lollygagging around when there was work to be done. He started by handling all those fix-up projects around the house that had needed attending for years. The *honey-do projects* - but without the honey, if his honey ever did come back.   Over the course of the last nine months, Jack had had to acknowledge that he might never win her back, no matter how hard he tried. There was a real possibility that he'd hurt Darla too deeply for her to ever recover. The absolute worst fight they'd ever had centered around his devotion to his mistress: work. Many stay-at-home moms would have been glad to have such a hardworking, devoted man. Not Darla, who demanded instead respect, kindness and in-person connection.

As a result, work had taken everything from Jack until there was little left over for his loving wife and delightful children. They'd reached the point where they were surprised to see him at all. When Jack did manage to make it home for dinner or to read the kids a story at bedtime, they were thrilled, almost as if Santa Claus had shown up. When he didn't

show up, Darla sought her own ways to pursue her dreams. She had started writing a novel, in fact, a romance about her own experiences as a highly sought-after young woman. Writing it made her feel good and even laugh, something she hadn't done much when Jack was off with his work-mistress.

Jack buckled down those first few days. After he fixed the water faucet in the guest bath, cleaned out all the gutters, and serviced the HVAC unit, he finally sat down and started doing some research. What would he do if he wasn't at Slocum & Grey Civil Engineers? He wasn't sure he could ever go back, given the shiver that ran up his spine every time he read the firm's name.

Jack perused the internet for hours, searching high and low. All he found were get-rich-quick schemes and paid 'consultants' who wanted lots of money to tell you how to get-rich-quick. Why could he find the information he needed? Why couldn't he get past the demands that he buy stuff? He forced himself to be patient. They had to sell advertising to stay afloat. He went back to his exhausting search for something, anything to do besides continuing down the lifeless track he'd chosen. Jack needed something he really *wanted to do*, not something he *had to do*.

After a while, Jack shut everything down. It was still early in the day. If he went into the city, maybe something would spark his imagination, give him a creative idea. He couldn't rely on internet searches controlled by some ad-bots. It would be great to be around other human beings. And the realization was starting to sink in: *if I don't learn to quit some of my habits, even the supposed good ones, I might lose my wife and kids forever.*

Jack was not in the habit of thinking like this. He was a concrete thinker, always focused on staying on budget and choosing between the lesser of two evils when seeking solutions for a major public works project. That was one of the ways in which he was so different from Darla. Everything she touched was accented by a splash of creativity, from making special lunches for the kids on holidays to crafting a scrapbook that looked as if a professional had made it. And whether she was writing a social media post, a card to a friend, or even the PTA newsletter, her writing was always fun, clever-

ly worded, and filled with useful, interesting information. As Jack thought about the differences between them, he became more and more acutely aware of what an amazing woman she was —which only made him miss her more.

Jack was on his way to the city in nothing flat, marveling at how easy it was to get a solo guy out the door. It had always been huge production to get a six-year-old, an eight-year-old, and their mother out the door. Something always got left behind, someone always had to use the potty one more time. Water, always water. Those kids couldn't go three blocks without someone dying of thirst. While Jack enjoyed the freedom to move about at will, he missed some of the contained chaos.

CHAPTER
15

I n the city, it took Jack almost an hour to find parking. He bit the bullet and paid $40 up front to park in a dingy garage. With no plan in mind, he started to wander the streets. At least he'd get in his 10,000 steps. After an hour, he wondered if he should be more intentional than just scanning the streets for inspiration. That's when he heard someone calling his name.

"Jack! Jack Hemet!" Jack felt instantly transported to his favorite deli as he turned to see Big Tony.

"I thought that was you!" shouted Tony as he walked towards Jack, arms open wide.

"Big Tony! What a treat!" said Jack, and the two friends embraced. Tony seemed emotional.

"Hey buddy, what's wrong?" asked Jack.

"I don't know, just sometimes, I'm just so emotional after my heart attack," he said, as Jack nodded compassionately.

"Yeah, I've heard that happens."

"So why are you in the city?" asked Tony.

"Doing some research, no big deal," said Jack.

"Have you had lunch?" asked Tony.

"Not yet," Jack replied.

"Let's go get something, my treat," Tony said.

Minutes later, they were standing in front of a sidewalk gyro cart. Jack had to laugh. It was so like Big Tony to find the best sidewalk cart food in the city. Tony handed Jack a gyro overflowing with lamb or pork or some type of meat, not that it mattered. It was delicious, and his pal Big Tony was buying.

"What brings you into the city today?" asked Tony, moaning at the goodness of the gyro.

"To be honest, I've hit my limit at my job. I want to try and spread my wings and, I don't know, maybe that means trying out another career. I came to the city just hoping to find some inspiration," said Jack.

Big Tony looked at his friend intently as a slow smile broke across his face.

"That's great, Jack. Takes balls. You can do it and hopefully get your family back together," said Tony.

"From your lips to God's ears. What're you doing here? I thought you were glued to that counter." said Jack.

"Yeah, yeah, I'm there a lot no doubt. Me and my whole family," said Tony.

"I didn't know your family worked there," said Jack.

"Oh yeah. My niece, Gina, she works in the bakery, my sons work the stockroom. My youngest buses tables, she's a hoot. Always chatting up the customers. My lovely bride, she minds the books, and then there's me," he said.

"Wow, a real family affair. I never realized. Must be nice," Jack said.

"You know, we have our ups and downs, but hey, we're together, and that's all that really counts in the end, hey?" said Tony.

"Yeah, so true," said Jack, mulling over how much he missed his butterfly kisses from Heather, and manly side hugs from Harry. "So what're you doing in the city?"

"I just came in to see my banker," said Big Tony.

"Really? Banker? For what?" asked Jack

"You're looking at Mr. Anthony Campanella, landlord," said Tony proudly. He explained how they had downsized their home, cashed in Tony's IRAs and 401(k) and invested much of the proceeds in a small apartment building.

"I'm not only the owner. I manage it, and I'm even the super when there's a clogged toilet! It's given me enough cash flow to buy another property, which I'm about to close on," said Tony. Jack nodded and listened, but the wheels in his brain started turning.

He knew a little something about real estate investing on a small scale. When his stepfather Leroy was close to retirement, he partnered with a fellow tradesman, a plumber, to buy a two-bedroom house in a low-income part of town. They fixed it up and rented it out for four years, eventually owning and renting six homes. The income supplemented their meager pensions and Social Security checks. Leroy wanted to go bigger. He almost did, making a deal to buy a twelve-unit apartment building but at the last moment, Jack's mother Mary talked him out of it. Everyone was grateful for her stubborn insistence because six months later, the market dipped badly. Leroy would have been upside down, with his properties losing 60% of their value overnight. Talk about dodging a bullet!

Because of that experience, Jack always thought real estate was a risky business. Real estate speculation had ruined many smart and ambitious men. But Jack also loved building things, especially renovating and revamping. He loved making things that were old, broken, and discarded new and useful again. And right now, that process seemed to mirror his life.

"Interesting," said Jack nodding. His mind was already racing into the future. He couldn't wait to start doing his research.

"Are you thinking about it, too?" asked Tony, seeing how Jack was lost in thought. "It's not for the faint-hearted. And you can lose, too, if you don't play your cards right."

"Okay, yeah, but where would I even start?" asked Jack.

"First, get your real estate license," said

Tony.

"Why wouldn't I just work with a broker?"

"Because you can save yourself a ton of money not having to pay those commissions. You get to know the different areas of town very intimately, and you know what they say–"

"Knowledge is king," they both said at the same time. Jack laughed and gave Tony a high-five. But before he could leave, Tony stopped him.

"Jack, if this is something you really want to do, remember, and I know this goes against your nature, you're gonna have to quit," he said.

"What does that mean?" Jack asked, bewildered.

"You're gonna have to tell everyone around you that yes, you're quitting a sure thing for a risky venture. You also gotta quit those nagging doubts that will pop up. They're definitely going to pop up, because I know you, and quitting will be very hard for you. You'll have to quit the disbelief that you are not savvy enough to pull this off. Because you are," said Big Tony gravely. Jack nodded, his heart started racing with a mix of fear and anticipation.

"Will you mentor me?" asked Jack.

"Of course I will!" Tony said, laughing. "Go get that license, and then we'll talk," and off Big Tony strolled to see his banker. Jack smiled and turned back to his car. His walk quickly became a run as he rushed toward his future.

CHAPTER
16

The next several days flew by as Jack found himself spending seven or eight hours a day doing his research. Knowledge may be king, but its prince is preparation. Jack drew on one his real strengths here, because he was always well prepared, whether it was for a client meeting or a presentation to the contractors. He even prepped for social engagements, plotting out what he might say, what bits of humor he might inject in the right situation.

His initial research introduced Jack to ways to shave costs by circumventing a pricey contractor, instead going right to subcontractors like carpenters, painters, and plumbers. After years of observing Leroy, he knew how to talk to them to get the best price and job. He knew what to look for when purchasing an investment property, like access to schools, shopping, and other key indicators. He still had lots to learn. He signed up for real estate school to get his license. That was a big step for Jack, one that meant a real financial commitment. It meant this endeavor was more than a whim. At his heart, Jack was cheap. Because this was going to cost him upwards of $700, it had to be worth it. If it wasn't, he wouldn't invest a dime.

He started driving neighborhoods to get to know them. First, he did his research. He started online with Zillow, Realtor.com and other sites where he could glean all kinds of useful information, from how long a home for sale was on the market to square footage and even the comps in the adjacent area. Nothing was more useful than actually driving a neighborhood. You could see firsthand if it was ragged or well-kept, and if it was close to shopping, a supermarket and other essentials.

He even got out and walked some neighborhoods. He got a couple of strange looks from people walking their dogs, but he just smiled and nodded and tried not to linger too long in one spot. Jack loved research, and he was surprised at how much fun this particular research was, way more fun than being hunched over a desk for 10 hours a day staring at engineering drawings.

Back in the car, he raced home and started doing all the research he could on each area. Jack began a detailed log of home prices, time on the market and other vital information for every house sold in the last year. He found it invigorating. For the first time in years, he felt as if he was taking back some control over his life. He couldn't wait to tell Darla.

He had to think about that. Yes, the first thing a guy does when he's excited about something is tell his best friend. That was Darla. She was not only his wife and mother of his children but his best friend. He'd always spilled all his fears, failures, and fortune out to her. She'd listen and nod. She didn't give him much advice, though, except to reassure him that he was a good man.

That was before the kids came along. Then things got busy. For Jack it was work, come home, go back to work. His life became a hamster wheel of racing home, eating leftovers from what could have been a happy meal with his family, taking in the local news, crashing, then getting up and returning to work. Period.

He had known even then, known in his bones, that his heartless life had to change. He had to change. He had to learn to quit. Quit all the white noise of being so committed to his job, quit thinking he had no choices and most of all, quit believing that the worst thing in the world was quitting something. Perhaps this new venture would be the key to starting

over and winning back his family.

Classes at the local junior college were fun. Jack was learning some basics about real estate and being a Realtor®. Though Jack thought the title "Real estate investor with a real estate license," might be a better fit for him. He had no intention of actually selling real estate to others for a commission. Of course, he would remain ethical because it was ingrained in him as much as the fear of being a quitter was.

The two weeks of Jack's vacation went by in a flash. He spoke to Tony several times, sometimes even twice a day. Tony seemed to relish the opportunity to mentor to his friend and to ensure Jack didn't make the same mistakes he did. Tony even started to dabble with the idea of beginning his own online course in Starting Small and Growing A Real Estate Portfolio. It was a fun time for both. When Jack realized on Sunday evening that he was supposed to return to work the next morning, he decided he'd need a few more days. With a large, wary gulp, he resolved to call Ms. Schneider the next morning.

Bright and early, after a brisk walk and a hearty breakfast, Jack took several deep breaths and phoned the office. The receptionist, who was happy to hear from him, put him straight through to Ms. Schneider.

"Jack, if you need a few more days, that's cool. How many are we talking?" she asked.

"I'm thinking Wednesday?" he said.

"This week or next?" she asked, a bit cautious.

"This week. I just need a couple of more days to wrap up a, um, a home improvement project I'm working on." That was not a stretch of the truth to Jack because, as he saw it, he was trying to repair his home life.

"That sounds good. See you Wednesday. Please come by my office when you first arrive, okay?" she asked.

"Sure, and thank you," said Jack. He was happy, but his stomach twisted at the idea of the HR lady wanting to see him. It felt a bit like being called to the principal's office in middle school. He turned back to the day's work, just a little nauseous.

CHAPTER
17

"He what?!" bellowed Arthur, giving Ms. Schneider a searing look. He wanted her to demand that Jack the feckless bum get back into the office to bail out Arthur's team. As a seasoned HR pro, Ms. Schneider did not change course. She barely even moved a facial muscle in response to Arthur's anger.

"I told him he could take a few more days if he needed them, and that's what he's doing. That's his right, and it's a contractual obligation between the company and Jack," said Ms. Schneider quietly. Arthur paced back and forth a couple of times before stopping close to Ms. Schneider.

"I have a good mind to fire him once he returns from his frickin'–" he said, searching for the right word, "sabbatical. And then we'll see who gets the last laugh." Arthur radiated the cockiness of a star high-school quarterback who's just thrown the winning touchdown pass. Ms. Schneider had to restrain herself from laughing.

"It is your department, and you have the power to hire and fire as needed, within your budget, of course," she said. "But firing a man who's saved this company's projects in countless ways, saved us frustration and money over the years, has sacrificed to make sure jobs are completed and on budget, well, that might be too smart. Firing him for taking the much-needed time he's contractually due might be a problem." She paused, hoping he'd finish the thought on his own. But Arthur was too on fire with anger to complete the thought.

"And what would that problem be?" he finally said.

"That would leave us open to a pretty hefty lawsuit, which Mr. Slocum and Mr. Grey would have to settle quickly. Of course, they'd need someone to scapegoat," she said. This gave Arthur pause. His face changed in a blink, and the redness in his cheeks subsided as he weighed his options.

"Okay, I get it, but,"

"Arthur, no 'buts' please. The simple fact is this. You have an entire team of people who are supposedly competent. If you're dumping all the extra work on one man, either your department is overstaffed, or the people you've hired are actually incompetent, or they're just mismanaged." She let that last word sit there.

Arthur blinked wide-eyed. Even he had to recognize the not-so-veiled threat.

"Yes, ma'am," he said.

"Would you mind closing the door on your way out?" she added, a smile of victory sneaking out. Arthur did as he was told.

CHAPTER
18

Jack was starting to seriously plot his escape. He knew it would be risky if he quit his day job and went into real estate. The very thought made him so nervous he had to walk around the block a couple of times, muttering calculations to himself like a madman. He was so animated, gesturing with his arms and hands to the point that a casual observer might think he was dueling with some unseen foe and call the cops. That was just his way of working out some of the conflicting issues bouncing around his brain.

Being called a "quitter" all those years ago had left an indelible mark. The vow Jack made as a boy, the one that he'd religiously observed, made him not only a good friend but also an excellent employee. It had also caused most of his bosses to add work to his schedule, exploiting his time and his brainpower to the point of exhaustion. He had collapsed every evening when he returned from work because he was so mentally and physically exhausted. His exhaustion left his wife, his kids, even the dog in second place, at best. He had no close friends, no charitable organization or church to attend, nor did he play golf or tennis like the other dads in the neighborhood. Jack just worked.

All this played in his head as he walked to the front door of Slocum & Grey. His heart was pounding, but he took solace that he'd get to see a friendly face in Ms. Schneider before he met with Arthur the madman. He greeted a couple of colleagues who seemed genuinely happy to see him, or they maybe were just relieved because they thought their workload was going to diminish big-time now that he was back.

At the door of Ms. Schneider's office, she waved him inside and gestured for him to sit down. "How was your time off?" she asked cheerily.

"Excellent. I got some projects done around the house, got to visit my kids several times and starting doing some research," he replied with a nervous smile.

"Oh, good. What kind of research?" she asked. Jack took a deep breath before responding. He knew that even though Ms. Schneider was friendly, her job was to make sure the company was properly staffed, and Jack leaving was going to cause somewhat of an uproar.

"On what I am going to do after I leave

here," he said. She looked straight at him with her best poker face. Inside, Ms. Schneider wanted to scream. She knew replacing someone like Jack was going to be virtually impossible. She calmly nodded.

"Maybe I'm not surprised. What are your intentions, Jack?" she said softly.

"Depending on a couple of factors, I am thinking about self-employment," he said.

"You do know that you're contractually bound if you leave to not pirate any of our clients," said Ms. Schneider sternly.

"Yes, I know. But don't worry. I've had enough of civil engineering. If I walk away, I don't ever want to look back," he replied. Somewhat relieved, Ms. Schneider got onto her computer.

"You'll want to know what your exit package would look like" she said, already looking it up.

"Yes, but, for now, this stays between just you and me, right?"

"Indeed. No one will know but me," she said.

"Good, because I have to have a couple of meetings before I make a final decision," he said. She looked at him with compassion.

"I hope whatever you're planning to do works out for you and whomever you need to meet with is on your side. I'll have something for you by end of day," she said. "Oh, and one last thing. Any idea when you'll actually make a decision?"

"I'd say in the next couple of days," he replied, standing to leave.

"Whatever you decide, I wish you the best of luck."

"Thanks. I'll need it."

No sooner had Jack reached his desk than Arthur was standing beside him, tapping his fingers insistently to express his dominance, not making eye contact — because clearly Jack wasn't significant enough to merit even a glance.

"My office. Now," said Arthur. He didn't wait for a response, just strutted off, knowing compliant Jack would follow. Michael saw this interchange and whispered as Jack walked by.

"Dude, I hope you made other arrangements while you were away. He is really pissed at you," said Michael. Jack just shrugged. The mere fact that he had options made his step a bit lighter. Still, he was not a lover of confrontation, and a confrontation was certainly coming.

"I'll be okay," said Jack as he headed into the lion's den. Arthur was sitting in his chair, facing away from the door, staring out the window.

"Close the door, and sit down," Arthur demanded. He couldn't see Jack's face. Couldn't see Jack was no longer afraid, no longer surprised, no longer intimidated, even though deep down a bit of nervousness still lingered.

"I'll get to the point, Jack. You ever pull a stunt like that again, your butt is toast. I'll fire you on the spot," said Arthur as he spun to face Jack, slapping the desktop for emphasis.

"Never pull that crap again on me, your team, or this company who's graciously given you a good job, or you're fired!" shouted Arthur. Jack sat silently, smiling. Arthur didn't get it. He gave Jack a quizzical look, his head cocked.

"Are you not hearing me, or are you just stupid?" asked Arthur. Jack winced at that.

"My hearing is just fine, last time I checked. And last time I checked, I was not stupid. But you know what I am?" asked Jack.

"What's that, hotshot?" said Arthur demeaningly.

"I'm due for another, oh, I don't know, six or seven weeks of paid vacation, is what I am. I think I'll take another day off, maybe the rest of the week," said Jack boldly. As he stood to leave, Arthur jumped to his feet.

"You walk out that door, you little weasel, and you're fired!" said Arthur with the smirk of someone holding a royal flush in a high-stakes poker game. Jack turned around.

"Okay," said Jack.

Arthur did not expect this response. Taken off guard, he stumbled back a little and plopped back down in the massive, leather chair, wanting to strangle this ingrate. Jack just stood there, unflinching, unmoving. Arthur realized how the loss of Jack could throw his department into utter chaos.

"Wait, wait, wait, wait, you know I was just joking. Just messing with ya, Jack. You're a much needed, very important cog in the wheel of this team's success, and I was just trying to, you know, put the fear of God into you, get it? Kinda funny, don't ya think?" said Arthur.

"No, I don't think you are funny at all," said Jack, "I'll see you later. Don't worry, I'll let Ms. Schneider know what went down."

Arthur was in a pickle now. He had waited two full weeks for Jack to return so he could dump six weeks of work on him as penitence for his outlandish behavior. Without Jack to pick up all the slackers' slack, how would the rest of his team ever get a break?

Jack was still walking away. He grabbed his jacket to leave. When Michael saw this, he started to panic, too.

"Jack, what the hell? Are you leaving again?"

"Yep, got some more things to do, so I need some more time off. I'll see you around," replied Jack. Michael was stunned. Across the office, heads began to pop up from cubicles like a giant game of Whac-A-Mole. Whispers started to flow through the space.

"Jack's leaving?" "What the hell?" "What're

we gonna do?" "We're screwed!" Jack heard them all. Yes, they were screwed. He was unfazed and kept walking. With a smile.

Michael followed him. "Jack, wait, what's come over you? I thought we were pals? Best work buddies. Listen, dude, you're needed. We really need you, we can't–" Jack cut him off.

"Yeah, you need me. But the only reason most of you even like me is because I do the work you were suppose to do and didn't. Everyone knows I cannot leave something undone. You all know I won't quit until hell or high water is flooding over me," said Jack, fighting to keep the resentment out of his voice.

"You thought I'd never speak up, never push back, do anything you ask while you go off to watch your kids play baseball or have a night off with your sweetheart or watching a tennis tournament you had to make 'cause the tickets were so expensive. All while my wife and kids were slipping away from me. Well, not any more, dude. Not any more."

With that, Jack walked towards the elevators. Arthur, watching from his office door, was stunned. Everyone was stunned. Jack was the rock of their department, if not of the entire company. To lose him would be like losing a limb.

Lori, the only female engineer in the firm, ran to catch him before he got on the elevator.

"Jack, wait!" she said.

"What?" said Jack, half expecting another lecture on his betrayal.

"I just want you to know, no matter what you do, you fight for those kids and you fight for your wife," she said with conviction. Jack wondered if she'd been through something like this himself.

"Thanks, Lori. It's been a pleasure to work with you," he said. He reached out to shake her hand and Jack was surprised to find Lori hugging him. He hugged back, long and hard. Then he pulled back, got on the elevator and went down, fighting tears.

CHAPTER
19

Once again, as if by muscle memory, Jack's car was heading east. After a few minutes, he stopped and texted Darla. And because this was a make-or-break moment, he did something he'd not done in years. Jack prayed.

"God, I know you don't hear from me very often. Like, in twenty-something years, maybe? It's Jack Hemet. Remember me? Of course you do. You're God. Anyway, I was wondering if you'd do me a favor, please, dear God. Soften Darla's heart towards me. I know she's mad and probably wants to divorce me, and for good reason, but I am just now understanding why." he said sincerely, "We took vows. I took a vow and I want to follow through on that so please, please, soften her heart." With that, he lifted his head and texted her. Darla responded. That was unusual, so perhaps God was already at work. Jack was as impressed as he was grateful.

He asked Darla if they could have a talk tonight if possible, maybe even over a glass of wine. To his shock, she agreed. Jack was excited. He knew this meeting would probably determine his happiness for the rest of his life. He swallowed hard and took off for Darla's favorite wine café.

When he pulled over to get some gas and coffee, Jack got a ping on his phone. It was from Ms. Schneider. Curious, he opened it.

"Dear Jack, I put this together and wanted to send it right away, as I know you decided to take another day for some personal time. Attached is a PDF of your exit package if you choose to resign from Slocum & Grey. Let me know your thoughts. Sincerely, Katharine Schneider."

Jack's first thought was not about his severance package but surprise that she actually had a first name. He opened the PDF and was about to drop the car into gear when his jaw dropped. What he read sent a shiver, the good kind, up his back.

"Wow, holy cow," He stopped himself from cursing, since the good Lord had already heard his prayer "This is unbelievable!" The possibilities of what this kind of money meant started to stir around in his head so wildly that he could hardly pull forward.

An annoyed driver behind him honked loudly, and that shook him back to the moment. As he drove out of the gas station and on to

Meadowridge, he went as fast as possible without breaking the speed limit. He wanted to fly there, to show Darla his good news, to promise her things would be different, and most of all, to let her know that he treasured her love and companionship more than any job, more than any promotion. He was almost floating off the seat, His heart was racing, and he was happier than he had been in years.

When Jack arrived, daylight was fading. He called Darla and she did not answer. He texted her. Nothing. Not sure what to do next, he just waited. Finally she texted him back: "Café Leon on 6th Street. Know it?" He texted back, "I will find it," and off he drove.

On the way, he almost stopped to buy her a bouquet of daisies, but he reconsidered. She might think it was manipulative and walk out. Darla was not one to play games. She was simple, direct, and honest, so he would be honest, too. Confession, they say, is good for the soul. His plan was to make his confession and to lay out his plan of action. He offered up another short prayer as he parked and walked to the café door.

Darla was already there when he arrived.

He walked up smiling, but his ear-to-ear grin faded a bit as he realized but she was barely able to raise a polite smile. Jack sat down. Perhaps the news he was about to give her would be perk her up a bit.

"Hey, thanks for meeting me in person," said Jack.

"Sure. What's up? What's so urgent that you couldn't just call me?"

"I've made some decisions and wanted to bounce them off you," he said.

"Why? You're a big boy, decide on your own," she said. She pushed back her chair as if she was about to leave, but Jack gently stopped her.

"Please, Darla, hear me out," he said. After a moment, she shrugged and sat back down.

"Okay, you've got three minutes, then I have to get going."

"Fair enough. Here's my truth. I am quitting Slocum and Grey, effective immediately," he said. Darla was too stunned to respond. She shook her head, hearing something that could not possibly be true.

"Say what?"

"I quit," he said. Darla had been wanting to hear those words for years.

"Um. Good for you. Hope it works out well for you," she said and started to leave again. Jack stood, stepping in front of her.

"Darla, don't you see? I did this for you and for the kids, our family," he said. He could see she was blinking back tears. She kept them all bottled up.

"No. I can't do this again. The promises, the lies, the 'I'll be home soon' tales and then, nothing. You're gone even when you're home. I don't want it anymore," she said emphatically.

"I hear you. I don't want it anymore, either. I understand what you've been saying all this time, and I've made a real commitment to change," he said.

"How so?" she asked, sitting down again. Just then, a brawny young man in a tight tee shirt interrupted.

"Is everything alright, ma'am?" he asked. Jack bristled.

"Yes, everything's fine, now can you please give us some privacy?"

"I wasn't talk to you, pal, I was talking to the lady," he said, getting tense.

"That lady is my wife and we're discussing our future, so thank you, but please leave." said Jack. Darla had never heard that much conviction from him before. She didn't know what to make of it.

Jack sat back down, cheeks flushed. "Now, where was I? Oh yeah, my confession. Yes, I was a good financial provider but I have not been there for you and the kids emotionally. I didn't spent time with you and Harry and Heather, not the time you deserved. I regret it all because, what's my life without the people I love the most?" he said. Darla was having a harder time fighting back the tears.

"Jack, I so want this to be true. I so want it, but…" she said.

Jack continued. "I am quitting first thing in the morning. Now I want you to see what I just received from HR. My financial package." He held up his phone to show her the PDF sent to him by Ms. Schneider. Darla looked at it for a second and her eyes got wide. She reached for her glasses and looked again.

"Jack, what is this? Is this your exit package?"

"It is. My plan, if you agree. I want to leave civil engineering altogether. I want to find something the whole family can get behind. Something that's healthy for all of us" he said.

"What are you thinking?"

"I've done my due diligence and think I want to, if you agree, buy houses, fix them up to either rent or sell. I want to start by downsizing our house, getting into something smaller, more cozy. Thoughts?" he asked.

Yes, she had thoughts, lots and lots of thoughts. A rush of emotions and memories and hurts and triumphs washed over her. She felt like she did on their first date. She wanted to puke, laugh, cry, and scream all at the same time.

He saw she was struggling so he put his hand over hers, "Are you okay?" Jack asked. She nodded. She couldn't bring herself to look him in the eye because she might burst out bawling like a baby. This was the one thing she had always wanted from him. to want her and the kids more than his job.

"Darla, all those late nights and weekends when I was working, I really wanted to be with you and Harry and Heather. You're my everything. It took me years, years to understand that quitting some things can be wise, it can be noble. I quit. Did you ever think you'd hear that from me? I quit! I want a brand new start, with you by my side," he said with more passion and conviction than she'd ever heard from him.

Darla didn't respond. Maybe he needed to explain his thoughts better? "My plan is to start investing, small at first," he began to say. She reached across the table and grabbed his face and kissed him hard, harder. They couldn't stop. She cried, he cried, everyone in the bar who was watching them cried, everywhere, everyone was crying. They all could hear the conversation. It was a small restaurant.

"I have waited so long, so very long to hear you say something, anything like this. I am so in love with you, please, please make sure what you're saying is true, please, don't disappoint us again," she said. He nodded and pulled away.

"Okay, well, let's do it," he said, pulling out his phone. Jack pulled up Ms. Schneider's email and hit reply. As he typed, he spoke his email out loud so Darla could hear what he was saying.

"Dear Ms. Schneider: I have decided in the best interests of my life, my marriage and my children to resign from Slocum and Grey. It's been a ride, and I am grateful for the employment. It's time to make this break. Please send all my personal effects to my home. Thanks for being kind to me and understanding my journey. Regards, Jack Hemet."

He hit Send.

"There, that's done." Darla grabbed Jack and kissed him again, and again.

"That's all we wanted, all we asked for was you," said Darla.

"I'm so happy I could dance," said Jack.

"No one should have to put up with that," cracked Darla.

And this isn't everything," Jack said. "We need to find a way for you to get back to your writing and creating. You're so talented. We can

set up an office for you." And Darla kissed him again, hard, lingering.

They stood to leave and the restaurant was filled with applause. "Bravo! Bravo!" filled the air. Some rose to their feet. "Bravo!"

Jack Hemet was finally a happy man. And to think, all he had to do was quit.

CHAPTER
20

A few days later, Darla and the kids moved back into the house. As soon as they arrived, Jack told the kids they would be moving to a smaller house not far away.

"Okay, but Daddy, will I still have my own room?" asked Heather. It was a legit question.

"Of course, it's not going to be that much smaller," Jack said, "but if we sell this now, we can make some serious…" Darla interrupted.

"She doesn't need all the details, Jack, just assurance," she said. Turning to Heather, she continued, "We'll move to a house close enough that you'll be at your same school and have your same friends."

"That's frickin' awesome," replied Harry. His parents scowled.

"What did I tell you, that Oscar kid, he's a rascal," said Heather. Jack and Darla had to stifle a laugh.

"Harry, we don't like that kind of language," said Jack. Darla crossed her arms and nodded in agreement.

"Oscar's my good friend," said Harry.

"No doubt, but your dad's gonna be home a lot more so we'll–" Darla began —but the kids were too excited to sit still.

"Really!? Oh Daddy, that's the best news ever!" shouted Heather as she jumped into his arms. Harry went to hug his dad, fighting back tears.

"That's awesome, Dad, really awesome," Harry said, patting him on the shoulder as he pulled away from his hug.

"Yeah, and I'll be working from home, too," said Jack. Harry cocked his head. "They're gonna let you do that?"

"Well," Jack said, looking at Darla and smiling, "we have some other news. I am not working for them any more." Heather was delighted but young enough that it didn't really sink in. Harry, on the other hand, was perplexed.

"Who are you gonna work for then?" asked Harry. Jack smiled.

"Me, and your mom, and the two of you." Again, Harry was confused.

"Your gonna work for…" Then it dawned on the boy "Oh, I get it! You're gonna work for yourself! That's great but doing what?"

"Oh a little of this and a little of that," said Jack, but Darla elbowed him.

"Don't be so secretive! Dad's gonna start a business buying houses, then fixing them, maybe selling them or keeping them to rent out, that sort of thing," she said.

"That's not exactly right. We, your mom and I, are going start a business together, because she'll be helping me pick the right house, the right neighborhoods, and she'll know how to make them look really good on the inside," said Jack.

"Mommy, you're super good at that!" said Heather.

"Show of hands, who thinks Mom is super creative?" asked Jack. Everyone raised their hands, except Darla, of course.

"She's going to start writing again. Her plays, her short stories. Maybe one day she'll be a famous writer," said Jack.

"Oh, don't be silly. It's for fun, and we'll see what happens," said Darla. With that, the kids went off to do homework as Jack and Darla

started dinner.

Jack and Darla set up their real estate venture to buy, renovate, and sell houses. Along the way, they kept a few for themselves to earn some residual income. It worked well for the first couple of years, as Jack was very handy and did a lot of the work himself. Of course, they hit a few snags along the way, like the time Jack installed the wrong water heater in a home and it burst and almost ruined the entire flooring!

As Jack likes to say these days, *experience is the best teacher*. Big Tony could not have been more proud of his protégé, and they talked at least once a week. Jack often took the family to Big Tony's for lunch on the weekends, and they always had a good time, laughing and telling stories with Tony and his tight-knit family. Eventually he became one of Jack's best friends.

Jack learned the trade quickly and was soon known around town as a decent man with good taste, which he attributed to Darla's decorator's eye. As he always said, he just provided the muscle. Within two years, they acquired and sold seven homes and put in a bid for an apartment building that needed some work.

Darla kept writing short stories and after submitting what seemed like hundreds (it was only twenty-three), she got one published. It was the thrill of her life. They all were happy and healthy.

As it turns out, God does answer prayers.

THE END

www.ingramcontent.com/pod-product-compliance
Lightning Source LLC
Chambersburg PA
CBHW051806050726
47598CB00006B/2448